I0171430

The Divorce and Doom of Simon Pastor

PETE DEAKON

In Fond Memory of Simon Pastor

July 20, 1981 – December 15, 2014

I miss you.

Author's Preface

Looking back, I am certain that in his last months with us Simon Pastor was aware that his journey's end was nearing. Those of us closest to him have since discussed the sadness his eyes betrayed no matter how large his smile during those last few months. And I, especially, feel a heavy burden because he once told me that when I tell his story ("and tell it you must!" he'd implore) that I need to get it right, that I need to share *everything*. In honor, then, of Simon Pastor's wishes I have chosen to write this book. His will granted me access to everything of his, including his laptop and phone. I have, of course, taken dramatic license with some parts of his story, but when you read a text exchange or email exchange, know that it is verbatim, typos and all.

1

Men get stuck. Simon Pastor was no different. Like every man he reached a turning point which defined all actions thereafter. Unlike some men, however, Simon fell prey to this moment. It overwhelmed him. It consumed him. And eventually it killed him.

Trauma is usually found within these turning points. I say trauma to emphasize the sheer shock of the event and its aftermath. Combat is the trigger for some, the senseless unexpected death of a loved one for others. For Simon, the event was his divorce.

When men are confronted by these moments, they respond in one of two ways. Either they grow or they get stuck. And I don't mean to imply that men have an equal chance of responding in either of the two ways, not at all. Most men get stuck. Most are not equipped with the skills and tools necessary to deal with the trauma. Poor Simon wasn't.

"Simon, here, is a virgin," said Brian. "He's holding out for his one true love."

Simon was, in fact, a virgin. But this did not make him any different from the rest of the eighteen year old college freshmen in the dorm room. The dorm room's dominant feature was the two twin beds lofted into the air by homemade wooden stands, which made the shape of an L in the corner. The room's current tenants each hung bed sheets from the ceiling in order to conceal any co-ed sports that may or may not occur on the beds. This was standard practice among the dorm's residents. The beds being in the air also created more space for the young men to come together for intimate conversations. In the case of Brian's room, this room, a love seat was under one of the beds. Two more 1950s style wooden desk chairs and one crummy bean bag chair completed the room's seating arrangement.

"You laugh," Simon replied, "but I actually did sign a 'True Love Waits' card once. With others, I walked it up to the front of the church during a special service and everything. A public vow between God and I. You ever made a commitment to anything higher than yourself before? Any of you?"

It's what we loved about Simon. He was honest to a fault and all heart.

"That depends on your definition of high, Simon," Chris offered to a general laughter among the guys.

Rolling his eyes and shaking his head, Simon took a breath.

"Is it on my back? My forehead?" he asked, pretending to wipe off a mark. "Why is it everywhere I go this is the most frequently discussed thing? No, I haven't had sex. Yes, I'd like to save myself for marriage. And yes, I'm proud of this and could not care less who knows. But I do hope that we can someday talk about something, anything, else," he lamented. "How about Josh? He was so drunk he pissed on his own computer the other night. Isn't that interesting?"

General merriment accompanied Josh's inadequate rebuttal.

For Simon, college was infinitely better than high school in every way save this one. In high school, while every boy talked about having sex, only a select few had actually gained carnal knowledge. In college, however, Simon soon found himself in the minority. And given the general lack of responsibilities that come with attending American universities, everyone soon knew.

He once shared with me, though, that almost to a man, when in a one-on-one conversation, the guys would admit that they respected him for his decision. I knew I did. It was not difficult to see why. Simon believed in principles. He believed in virtue. And that is rare.

2

Simon was no saint. It will become abundantly clear that he had a nasty brutish side. And we must never forget, of course, that he was first and above-all human. I say this to introduce the idea that he found himself approaching his twenty-fourth year of virginity with a tiresome weariness. It had been years since he attended a church service and despite plowing through books on religion, the memory of the *why* of it all was fading.

The fall after he turned twenty-four Simon learned that his friend Kurt was getting married. Kurt asked him to be his best man and Simon figured he may as well learn how to dance for the occasion. He first heard Kerri's name as the dance studio's receptionist told him who his instructor would be.

"We do private lessons on Wednesdays, so Wednesday night at 8pm you'll be with," the woman paused as she checked the instructor availabilities, "you'll be with Kerri."

"Kerri. Got it. Great. See you then," Simon said. "I hope she's hot," he thought, after hanging up the phone.

He had scheduled lessons with high hopes of impressing the bride's single friends. Simon happily admitted to anyone who would listen that the many ballroom scenes within the recently finished epic *War and Peace* had a hand as well.

For some men a woman's smile is the most visible memory of first seeing her. Others can't forget her eyes. Many find themselves drawn to a woman's unadulterated laugh. Simon never forgot Kerri's posture. Arriving a few minutes early for the lesson, he saw a woman who he hoped would be Kerri. She was walking from left to right when their eyes first met. She was expecting him, but didn't expect *him*. The way Simon recounted it, she froze solid upon sight of him—her slender neck almost breaking in the violence—though Kerri would coyly never admit to being overly impressed with her future husband that day. He confided to me that he knew in that moment that she was the one. When I pressed him to explain how he knew, he admitted it was very primal. He said that he could just tell that she would give herself to him. Kerri was like that. Her body housed her spirit but was never very good at concealing it.

Too soon, Kurt's wedding had come and gone and the dance lessons lost their relevance to Simon's ambitions. Over the duration, however, Simon and Kerri had become quite close. As is often the case with new love, neither of them wanted to stop being around the other. Simon simply couldn't believe he had found a female that he'd like to have as a friend.

Simon had an uncanny ability to focus on a goal. Since signing that blue oversized "True Love Waits" index card, he viewed all available women as potential wives. Despite viewing marriage as an undesirable institution, he saw no value in befriending a woman who would someday choose another man. If he was going to spend time with a woman, he concluded, it had to be one he wanted to marry. And here she was, slightly tipsy, leaning against his car outside of the restaurant that he had taken her to after his last lesson. Not having any experience to aid his assessment of the unfolding drama, he returned to his safe place—honesty.

"Well, unless we're going to go somewhere else, I think this is it, Kerri," he struggled to say.

"Nope, I have no place to be," she said.

"Oh. It just seems like you're," he paused, searching for the most accurate word, "waiting for something."

"I guess-," she began.

"Plus, aren't you cold just standing out here?" he interrupted.

"-I was going to say we could go make out in your car," she said, laughing at his genuinely surprised reaction to her suggestion, "if that's okay with you."

"Hmm," said Simon as fear swept over him. Simon had never really made out before. But it sounded fun.

"Okay. Give me a second to open your door though. It doesn't work from the outside," he said, consciously moving as slow as humanly possible so as to not give away his excitement. Any restaurant staff still cleaning up inside who by happenchance had been peeking out at the scene would have thought Kerri had put a time limit on the offer Simon moved so fast.

Once inside the car, it didn't take Kerri long to conclude Simon was in uncharted territory, and she laughed as she told him as much. He, in turn, loved both parts of that. She was perceptive and unafraid. Only later did he remember she was also a little drunk. By the end, Simon had told me a hundred times if he told me one time that he always wondered how the relationship would've played out if it wasn't so late, if they weren't far from both their homes, and if it hadn't have been that time of the month.

As amazing as the evening had been, Simon was too much a boy scout to not regain control and come up for air.

"Call me when you get to your place. Drive safe," he said.

"I will."

Playfully pulling him towards her car, she managed to convince him that just a few more shivering kisses wouldn't hurt.

3

Simon once told me that his mom's "birds and bees" talk included a single assertion: "Just be careful. When you're alone with a girl on a bed, there are a lot of pressures." Rather vague, but true nonetheless I guess.

Three days later, a Friday, Kerri found herself driving to Simon's place after work. He lived closer to the studio than she did, so they figured that to increase the length of the date she would stay the night as she had to work the next day. It might seem odd—might not—that Kerri would so readily trust Simon. But in those three days, she had listened to him explain that he wasn't a good kisser for lack of practice, which led to the most startling and pleasant thought Kerri had ever contemplated. Simon was a virgin.

While Simon loved the feeling of respect he got in private from even the most publicly outspoken male mockers upon the discovery of his status, the truth was he was never prouder than when he heard the loudest pause on the other end of the phone as Kerri attempted to withhold her shock. This was followed by a giggle normally reserved for discovering buried treasure.

"Hey, Simon," she said as he opened the door.

"Hey."

They kissed.

"Okay, before anything else, like I said on the phone, I know it's weird, but I have to wash my feet," Kerri said. "Trust me."

It would have been impossible for Simon to feel more trusted and respected. She'd never even been in his apartment before, and yet he leaned against the doorway and watched as she sat on the side of the bathtub, running warm water over her bare feet.

Towel dry complete, the easiest of conversation continued and paved the way for innocent laughter. And then they touched. Freed from a car's inherent space and comfort restrictions, they touched a lot. The hour grew late enough that the pair decided to move from the couch to the bedroom. She turned away as she changed her shirt, momentarily exposing her back and the slightest outline of her naked left breast. Then she quickly swapped jeans for pajama pants, never removing her panties. Simon just watched. Something told him this was thrilling for her. Once in bed, they attempted to sleep for about five seconds before roaming hands and lips insisted that it wasn't bedtime. They alternated top and bottom as their elbows ached and knees burned. She encouraged boldness and finally he took off her shirt but nothing more.

He laughed as they shared a protein shake at about four in the morning. Not having thought through any part of the evening, certainly not expecting it to so naturally develop in this way, he was only modestly embarrassed that he didn't really have any food at his place. Placing the shaker cup under the running faucet, he filled it up about half way. Cutting the water, he replaced the cap. His entire body shook as he rinsed the shaker cup. He was proud to display an innocent vulnerability. Removing the cap and putting both cap and cup under the flowing water once again, he smiled at Kerri as he left the cup and lid to drain in the dish-rack and declared, "Clean!"

She laughed at his confidence while silently vowing never to drink another sip from that cup again.

When morning finally came, Simon treated Kerri to coffee and bagels at the nearby bagel shop. They walked briskly together on that chilly December day. He held the door open for her.

Bagels never tasted so good.

After she finished her Saturday shift, Kerri returned to Simon's place. While she showered, he waited on the couch. Happy to have her comfy pajama pants back on, she climbed on top of him. Once again, hands caressed, tongues slid, and hips ground. Not having a television, the sounds of lust were accompanied by selections from his late 90s cd collection. Eventually, some rapper said something about a blowjob.

"Do you want that?" she asked, pulling her lips away from his.

"Want what?" he replied, not quite believing his ears.

He watched her head remain still as her eyes turned towards the music. Then her head completed the turn and nonverbal hint. Believing that she made her point, she turned her attention back to him and smiled when she saw that his eyes understood. He felt the back of her fingers on his stomach and his waistband tighten against his lower back.

"You want to do *that?*" he asked.

She nodded.

"Uh," he stuttered, "okay."

****

She explained that he needn't be embarrassed. She said that it was probably because he had an erection for over twenty-four hours.

But he was.

"You probably don't want to kiss me now that I had your wiener in my mouth," she said, laughing.

Simon laughed and said, "Come here."

The next morning, Sunday, he got a call from a co-worker asking how the weekend was going, asking how late Kerri had stayed Friday night.

"Well, uh, she's still here," Simon happily reported.

"Way to go, bud. So you did it?"

"No, it's not like that," Simon clarified.

"She's been there two nights and you haven't fucked her?" Clint asked, not able to hide his astonishment.

"Jesus! When you put it that way it sounds like we've been having a miserable time. Not everyone is like you man. We've just been hanging out."

"Sorry man. Didn't mean to offend you. Just can't believe someone like you exists," Clint said. "Well, don't let me keep you. See you tomorrow."

"Thanks for checking in. Have a good one."

****

Climbing into bed with Kerri for the third night in a row, Simon thought he was doing pretty good. Climbing into bed with Simon for the third night in a row, Kerri feared that if she didn't make her move, he might lose interest before they could see each other again. So make her move she did.

"Ahhh," he said, gritting his teeth and pulling in a breath. "I just don't know Kerri. This has all been unreal."

Hurt, but not fully deterred, she soothed, "I'm not saying we have to. I just really want to and am able now."

They laid silent, both on their backs, both staring up at the dark ceiling.

"Fine. Let's do this."

A rush unlike any other she had felt came over Kerri as she watched him kneel at her feet and pull her underwear down the length of her lean legs. Next, Simon hopped off the bed to grab a condom. The anxiety kept him less than fully hard, but he got it on. Once inside her, he did his best to pleasure Kerri, but he couldn't believe how the condom prevented all sensation. Maybe it was because of the late hour, maybe it was simply nerves, but he swore he wasn't even inside her. Looking down in the darkness, he confirmed the ridiculousness of the thought, but still something was not right. Then he couldn't *not* think about how this was not at all like he imagined it would be. And, of course, as so often is the case, again, he couldn't finish.

Again, she didn't hold it against him.

Ten minutes later he began anew, this time no condom. She welcomed the effort with open arms. About as out of tune with himself as possible, Simon knew he didn't want to pull out until he was sure he would climax. And yet he knew the risk involved. So he split the difference.

Climbing off the bed to grab a towel, he reported, "That was the dumbest thing I've ever done."

Simon watched as anger chased the sadness from Kerri's face, and he realized what a terrible thing he had just said.

"I didn't mean that. I'm sorry. I don't know why I said it. I think it was because we just did what everyone who unintentionally has a kid does and we're smarter than that. Really. It was good. Better than good. It was great. You were great. Thank you," he fired off, hoping that a higher volume of shorter expressions would prove more potent than a long explanation.

Her anger subsided. She kissed him as they stood naked next to the bed.

4

A seemingly unending list of practical considerations appeared and within the month Kerri had moved in to Simon's one bedroom apartment. The apartment was located in the southeast part of a city known and respected for its ability to withstand suburban sprawl and retain its southwestern aesthetics. Simon chose the complex because it was one of the only ones in town that resembled the suburbia he had been raised in. The second floor apartment was accessible by a single outside cement staircase so familiar to unmarried men and women living in his time. Besides a laundry basket of her clothing, Kerri contributed a new set of high thread count bed sheets that wouldn't thrash their knees so bad.

Simon's schedule was more flexible than Kerri's fairly fixed one at the studio, and when possible Simon would sit outside on the stairs and wait for Kerri after she called to say she was on her way over after work. Simon would see her smile as she leaned forward while still in her car to look and see if he was there. That smile revealed how much she enjoyed being the center of Simon's focus. For his part, Simon loved treating her like the woman of his dreams. And she was the woman of his dreams.

It is true that Simon wasn't entirely comfortable with Kerri's profession. While he was, in fact, the second student (a co-worker of Simon's named Jake was the first) to capture her attention enough to break the studio's "no fraternization" policy, Simon felt remarkably special. This stands repeating. Perhaps it's ego, perhaps simple vanity, but there is something to be said for the feeling a man gets when he is selected by a woman who comes in constant contact with men. Not the best woman for a jealous man clearly, this type of woman can still make a man feel tremendously special. In effect, he tells himself, "She didn't choose him, him, him, him, him, him, him, or him. She chose me."

"Wait, who are we talking about?" Simon asked.

"You know. That guy that Hope sleeps with occasionally," Kerri answered.

"Right. The one that she essentially grinds on in front of everyone at the studio. I remember. What about him?"

"Well, he almost let the cat out of the bag today. Pretty funny and stupid at the same time. I think the owners know, but if he keeps it up, they won't be able to ignore the situation any longer," Kerri said. "And Hope can't afford to lose this job. She has a kid and is hoping to save up enough to open her own studio."

"You think she has the discipline to do that?" he asked.

"I think so. I mean, she has a wild side, for sure. But who doesn't?"

"Me?" he answered.

"Of course you don't. But you know what I'm saying."

"I guess. This is the same girl that joined the mile high club on the return flight from one of your work trips?" he asked, attempting to stay less than obvious with his opinion of her.

"I should have never told you any of this."

"Babe, I'm just saying that I don't think this woman should be given too much credit. Sometimes I get the feeling you measure yourself against her," he went on. "That's a competition I don't want you to win."

"Well, when Andy is not at the studio, who should I talk to? You can't expect me to not socialize at work," she said.

"Whatever. That's not what I'm saying at all. I just think that the people you surround yourself with influence you. You even said that when I first walked in to the studio Hope saw me first and told you a big white guy was your next student. Do you think you would've been so taken with me if she hadn't said that? Or if she had said I was ugly?"

"Okay. That's not fair. That's not fair at all. I'm done."

"Hey. I'm sorry. You have told me that you're easily swayable, and I don't like thinking about you doing something you'll later regret. You know I'm not going anywhere, right? I just don't want to be made out to be a fool."

His sincerity disarmed her completely. Closing the distance between them entirely, she let her lips brush his cheek as they made their way to his ear where she whispered, "You would have to be a fool to go anywhere, wouldn't you?" She lifted his shirt off his waistline and fumbled to undo his belt.

5

Soon enough Valentine's Day was upon them. Simon had never had a girlfriend, let alone a girlfriend on the best day to have a girlfriend. Kerri was an excellent dancer and wanted to go dancing after work. Simon had only had a few lessons. Practically this meant that Kerri would drink and dance the night away, and he would drink and watch. Of course she would dance with him as much as he wanted, but he knew it was painful for her, so he didn't ask often. Other instructors were going to the club, and he could stand watching her dance with women. He felt compelled to let her dance with a few male instructors as well, against everything his gut told him. So, while his stomach turned at the thought of spending his first Valentine's Day with a girlfriend on the sidelines, Simon agreed that it would be fun.

In the car, Kerri looked at her phone and reported that her friend Hope was already at the club. Seeing it was after nine o'clock at night, Simon shuffled back and forth impatiently while he waited for Kerri to change into her dancing shoes at the back of the car. She was always very particular about her feet.

Once inside Kerri disappeared with Hope as Simon headed to the bar to order their drinks. One of the few salsa clubs in town, seating was limited and soon an out of breath Kerri squeezed in next to Simon and followed her smile with an excited eyebrow raise. He couldn't match her enthusiasm.

"You okay, Simon?" she asked.

"Yeah. I just kinda wish I could dance better so that we could have fun. Watching you dance with Hope is only so satisfying."

"Do you want to dance with me? We can do the merengue. That's an easy one."

"Na," he answered. "I don't need pity. I'll hang here. Just go have fun," he said, hoping to sound mature.

Several high-tempo songs later, she returned to his side. She ran her fingers through her hair in an effort to pull free the few strands that stuck to the side of her face. He handed her a drink. He hadn't moved much while she was gone and wasn't moving much now.

An older, friendly looking man on their left commented, "Looks like you're getting quite the workout tonight."

Not needing to be a part of this and having been glued to their drinks and seats all night, Simon announced, "I have to go to the bathroom. Will you watch my drink?"

"Sure," Kerri answered.

Simon returned just in time to hear Kerri thrilled to be able impress the stranger with correct pronunciation of kinesthetic proprioception.

"Kinesthetic what?" the man asked.

"Kinesthetic proprioception," she repeated, delighted. "It basically means being able to control your body."

The man turned to Simon.

"You've got quite a woman on your hands, friend."

"Don't I know it?" Simon answered coolly.

Simon, like some men, preferred to keep the hurt inside than be viewed as socially inept. His stomach turned over and over as he sat listening to Kerri deliver all the lines that so captured his attention just a few short months before.

****

"As long as I get laid tonight, she can say whatever she wants," he rationalized.

She nearly fell asleep on the drive home. He let her go to the bathroom before he made his move. It took more words than he thought it should have, but he eventually won out.

Not quite a week later and after she consented to one condition, he asked her to marry him.

She said yes.

6

Is it so incredible to believe that a man could grow to age twenty-four without knowing hurt? But that's what I'm asking you to believe. Simon Pastor had lived under a protective shelter his entire life. No one had hurt him, and if he had ever hurt anyone up to this point, it was out of ignorance.

Simon never wanted to live where he grew up. To him, the suburbs were far too restrictive. He was quick to lead or join the chorus of anti-suburbanites who detested the cookie-cutter housing, keep up with the joneses mentality, and harshly implemented rules-of-decorum about everything that didn't matter.

When he finally moved away for good after college, sure, there was sadness. But there weren't tears. He had only been living with his folks between semesters and during the holidays. No one expected him to hang around. No one expected him to change his mind.

All this is to say that when Kerri cried and cried the day they drove away from her home town, he was uncertain how to act. On the one hand, he felt loved because she was choosing him over her previous life, but he also felt like maybe she wasn't really wanting to leave. The truth, of course, is that Kerri felt all those feelings and more. Home is a special place for just about everyone. Leaving it is never easy. Trading the desert for the beach should've made it easier, though, Simon thought.

A new job, new career, and new town all added to life's regular stressors. Simon wanted Kerri to be happy and saw that she wasn't. The summer passed as quickly as any before it, and her parents even made a trip across the country to visit her and Simon and see their daughter's new home.

Simon's job required a certain amount of travel, and a big three month trip was rapidly approaching as the year drew to a close. Despite being an incessant planner in nearly every facet of his life, Simon just didn't plan this relationship out. While Kerri had agreed to never cheat on him, he was getting nervous. Three months was going to be a long time apart. And everyone knew that loneliness and opportunity could make a fairly strong argument that the engagement was meaningless.

Simon was not concerned with any of the many statuses of a relationship. Whether Kerri was his girlfriend, fiancé, or wife, she was with him and he with her. What did it matter the title? He wasn't blind to Kerri's hopes and needs though. Soon he saw the opportunity to get married on the one year anniversary of their first meeting. He figured it was romantic in a way. So on one warm November day, Simon and Kerri drove to the municipality and became man and wife.

7

Before November came to a close the newly married Simon and Kerri found themselves lying in bed, trying to stay awake until the very last minute before he had to leave on his three month long trip. They dozed off for a torturously brief two hours before an alarm sounded at four in the morning. Unsure of when his next opportunity to shower might be, Simon walked to the bathroom and lifted the faucet handle up and to the left. The warm water hit his right foot first. Kerri sat on the lid of the toilet, not wanting to miss out on their last moments together. Stepping into the shower, he closed his eyes and turned his face into the water. He cried.

****

Kerri kept herself fairly busy while he was away. Most of the activity was during the day and she didn't have much of a nightlife. That made Simon happy. She didn't mind it either, as she knew that he worried about such things. It also afforded them time to talk on the phone each night. What Kerri didn't know, what she couldn't have known, was that while he was away and alone, an unrecognized hurt began to fester in Simon. She didn't know because Simon didn't know. He simply lacked the experience to process what he was feeling.

"Jake is such a douche," Matt declared. "He thought he could game the system, but he lost."

"For sure," Jason answered. "He was never any good at performing under pressure either. Nobody liked working with him."

The men sat at their computers, some reclining all the way back in their office chairs as they aimed their bored barbs directly at this Jake. Simon sat in on the conversation about Kerri's former boyfriend and pretended to not be interested. But he couldn't hear enough of it.

"Before we left for this trip, I actually ran into him. He has braces now. He's in his thirties and has braces," Matt repeated, believing his point was clear. "I just wanted to tell him 'dude, no girl wants to sleep with you.'"

It was true that Jake had braces. Simon had seen them himself. And while these men knew Kerri was Simon's woman, Simon wasn't sure whether they knew she had dated Jake. He decided adamant denial should be his course if the time came. Imagine his torment then. Were the men actively goading him? Were they just boys being boys? Whatever the situation, Simon was miserable. During that night's phone conversation he let Kerri know. She cried as she explained to Simon, yet again, that seeing Jake was all a big mistake. She cried as she explained that it was years ago and that now she was completely committed to Simon.

"I still don't understand what you ever saw in him," Simon said, unrelenting. "Do you know what it's like to have to listen to them talk like that about you?"

"Then why did you marry me?" Kerri yelled, tears still falling.

"I guess I didn't think it through," he asserted in full control of himself. He aimed to wound. He was hurting and he wanted her to hurt too. It didn't matter the reason or perpetrator. It didn't matter that she wasn't responsible for his hurt. Simon just wanted company.

Completely shut down, and yes, hurt, Kerri gave lip-service to a closing declaration of love and hung up the phone. For his part, Simon felt like vomiting.

8

Work was not going well and Simon was not quite able to ever break out of his misery. In a way, he was doing his dream job, but that only made it worse. People expected him to be happy, but he wasn't. As the breadwinner, not to mention that technology had made it easy, Simon arranged for automatic bill pay while he was away. Anything to make Kerri's life easier, he thought. But even this added to the stress. While browsing the phone bill, he noticed in the list of outgoing calls on and around Valentine's Day that there were a few calls placed to area codes from Kerri's home town.

"This damn holiday is going to be the end of me," Simon muttered as he picked up the phone.

He was never one for small talk, so despite only having fifteen more days before he saw her, he opened the conversation with uninformed accusations.

"I was checking the phone bill today," he volunteered. "Who'd you call from your home town?"

"What?" Kerri asked, confused. Rapidly joining the mood she answered, "Jesus. Are you serious? No 'How's it going?' No 'I miss you.' Just straight to jealous bullshit? When are you going to grow up?" she asked, ready to hang up the phone. Perhaps it was purely the intellectual concept that Simon, not her, was the one away from home. Perhaps it was kindness. Knowing Kerri, I'm confident that it was simply love that kept her on the line.

"I called my grandma. My grandma Simon. Is that okay? This is her first Valentine's Day without her husband. She's all alone and in her eighties, as you know. So I called her to say Happy Valentine's Day," she said.

Simon was so sure she had called an old fling, so sure.

"I'm sorry," he said. "I'm sorry. I just," he stopped. More common than either of them wanted to admit, their phone conversations had been fights. Sorry made more appearances than love. Explanations of why forgiveness should not be viewed as weakness were more frequent than tenderness and compassion.

He was so sure.

He began again, "Look. We're almost through this. Let's not talk so much for the next two weeks."

That is not what she wanted. She didn't know what to do, but knew she couldn't handle much more distrust. She agreed that it would be best that way. She knew Simon was a powerful man, and she sometimes had a difficult time distinguishing the world he saw from the world she saw.

Simon was convinced he wasn't the man all those phone conversations revealed him to be. Maybe he was right. But the man on the phone was the one who was coming home. He knew this. Kerri knew this. What should've been an exciting moment was instead a cautious one. Perhaps it was foolish for Simon to believe a couple could make it a lifetime without mechanical physicality, but for certain he never expected to be the cause of it.

For two years Simon and Kerri repeated the same cycle. He would be away for months at a time and his phone calls left Kerri feeling hurt. During the months he was home, Simon was able to mend some of what he ruined. But then he would leave again.

Finally Simon returned from a trip for the last time. Kerri and Simon had dreamt of this moment for over a year, but a lot had been lost over the years. Whatever Kerri thought, Simon knew he was the one who had taken it. He told me that it was difficult for him to pinpoint the moment that he knew he was at fault, but would always say that if he had to guess it was that second Valentine's Day—day seventy-seven.

9

"Time is always against us," Simon said once. He wasn't being philosophical. He meant that for Kerri and him there was never time for proper healing. In the same way that the body's joints never fully heal because complete rest is impossible, Simon's initial hurt never fully healed. Not that it was always exposed and raw, it just was never able to form scar tissue. And he had some abnormality which prevented him from being content to be the only one experiencing hurt.

"I kinda like it," Simon said. "What do you think?"

The rental house was nearly everything they wanted. It was away from work and that meant they might be able to finally make friends with the locals instead of co-workers. It had a backyard with a fence which meant Kerri could finally get a dog. And it was the least expensive place on the realtors list, which, in turn, meant more money for fun.

"I'm game. You know me. I'm the passenger on these things," she said.

She was right. Simon had given her the nickname passenger back when they had met, even before they were married. Kerri was fine with whatever. Simon viewed that as a strength to their relationship, but, of course, also the greatest weakness. If she let him drive so easily, he always feared she might take a ride with another.

In probably the smoothest move ever completed in the history of man, a few days later they were nearly unpacked. While not official homeowners per say, they sure felt grown-up. The three bedroom two bathroom single family home had more than enough room. The landlord had the singular goal of ensuring it was never vacant, which explained the low monthly rate. There was a pecan tree in the back, which no one realized would be as much work as it was. The yard was plenty big, and with the salary raises coming in steady increments, Simon was excited to buy a good lawnmower. Excited, until he walked behind it.

"What was I thinking?" he said, coming in after the chore was complete.

"What's that, Hon'?" she asked.

"Oh nothing. I just will never cease to be amazed at how I build up things. I really thought I would like mowing the lawn with a good mower. But it is horrible. I hated mowing the lawn as a kid and I still hate it now. We should've just bought a crummy used mower and spent the leftover money on liquor," he said.

"Yeah, well, a lot of good that idea does us now," she said. "You gonna be able to deal with it?"

"Sure. I'm just not happy about it. Please, please, please, please never let me forget that I hate mowing the lawn. Please."

Not looking up from the movie she was watching, she said, "Got it. You don't like to mow the lawn."

Soon enough they had their dog. It was a nightmare.

Everyone knows that after a couple gets a dog, a baby is only a year or so away. Simon and Kerri were no different. Initially Simon was not big on the idea of a child, but with the relationship stagnating, he figured it might not be a bad idea. Plus, he always kind of had it in his mind that no one should go their entire lifetime without creating another person and dealing with all the results of that decision.

As much as he possibly could, Simon preferred to hold a sober attitude when it came to big life events. He credited Hollywood for this outlook. Film after film put on display perfectly acted scenes of the pregnancy test proving positive. Couples were thrilled to tears, or women were angry as hell. For Simon, a positive test result was no surprise. Kerri and he decided to make a baby. They stopped all birth control. Kerri became pregnant. Sure it was exciting, but the god-awful truth was there was a long perilous road ahead.

One thing that made conversations with Simon great was learning how individual moments in time affected him absolutely. In the case of pregnancy, he told everyone that his view was formed after a single conversation with the boss at the pizza place job he had had in high school.

"So Laura already had little Sean when you married her, but Zach is yours, right John?" Simon asked John, one slow evening at the restaurant.

It was a family owned business and was Simon's first real job. John was the manager and that is an understatement. There had never been a better man for the position of managing high school students and all the associated drama. John had a presence that even Simon's parents couldn't forget after seeing how he handled a night of repeated mistakes on their order years earlier. Little did this John know that all those wasted mushrooms would lead to a great friendship.

"That's right, Simon," John said, trying to not lose count of the pizza boxes he was inventorying with pen and paper on a clipboard. "Sean is Laura's son and Zach is my son. Our son."

John taught Simon that the best way to ensure the inventory is accurate was to zig-zag the pointing pen as you count. If all the pizza boxes are stacked high, start by pointing at the top left box, and move towards the bottom right for a few boxes, then back to the left etc. Go straight down and you'll lose your place.

"What was that like?" the sixteen year old Simon asked. "The movies make it seem like it's the happiest moment a human can ever experience."

"Happiest moment ever?" John repeated, slightly annoyed that the subject matter required him to stop counting. "No, Simon. It isn't the happiest moment ever. It is probably the scariest. All you do is worry. Is my wife okay? Is the baby okay? Is it even possible to know that the baby is okay?" Simon's unabashed expression must've been a bit too much for John, and so he back-peddled a bit. "That isn't to say that I wasn't excited, but the movies are wrong."

And so it was that Simon received the news of Kerri's pregnancy with a simple smile and a semi-forced hug and kiss. They were on their way.

10

Of course John had been right. Simon knew this was going to be the case by the care which John had used when instructing him about an embarrassing truth. Now as he watched the nurse carefully—lovingly—use the purpose-built faucet to rinse off Emily's nearly bald little head in the sink of the hospital room, he was more than certain.

Simon had driven an overdue but not in labor Kerri to the hospital only eight hours earlier. The doctors had said that they would start a twelve hour long process of preparing to induce labor, which might then last another twelve hours. Kerri managed the discomfort of a few early contractions without much ado. It was easy for her to not focus on pain when a bigger fear loomed. Simon knew that she was only thinking one thing, and he tried to push the thought out of his mind because unlike most of life, he had no control over whether a C-section would be required.

"If you're doing alright, why don't you start that movie we brought while I go run and grab us some food. I think we're going to be in for the long haul," Simon offered.

Kerri didn't want to be left alone.

Just then a nurse came through the door; the doctor appeared soon after. The nurse annotated some measurements the machines recorded while a doctor that Simon and Kerri had never met before introduced himself as he checked Kerri's dilation.

"So we're going to induce labor now," the doctor announced.

Kerri and Simon's eyes opened fully as they stared at each other.

"Oh," Simon finally said, to the confusion of the doctor. "I thought we were taking this thing slow?"

"Nope, there's no need. It's time to get this baby out."

"Whatever you say doc."

"Please, please, please don't need a C-section," Kerri thought.

It should need no explanation why Kerri was afraid, but it does. While a medical marvel that has saved countless lives, mother and baby, there is an undercurrent of thought that

Simon and Kerri became aware of during the pregnancy. The thought being that C-sections were unnatural. Natural birth's brutal totality, all the pains and pressures, had a physiological reason, some said. The woman's body needed to experience them to fully recover after the child was born. A C-section was just a surgical procedure. No endorphins were released, no adrenaline, the song the broken record played. At least not in the same way. And then, to top it all, all of Simon and Kerri's peers constantly reminded them how much more money a surgeon makes for a C-section than for a natural delivery.

The nurse re-entered the room.

"Let's have you turn on your side, dear," she said to Kerri.

Turning over to her side, Kerri asked, "Everything alright?"

"Oh yeah. We're just trying to make sure baby is getting everything baby needs."

"You okay, Kerri?" Simon asked.

"Yeah. I think I'm feeling more contractions, but yeah."

The door opened again, the nurse seemed to walk a little faster.

"Let's put one of these pillows," she stopped and just readjusted Kerri's pillow herself. "There. How are the contractions? What number would you give them?"

"Seven or eight?" Kerri answered.

"Still not wanting an epidural?" the nurse asked.

"Honestly, if it's going to actually get much worse, I am going to need one."

"Okay, dear, I'll tell the doctor."

Epidural complete, the surgeon returned and explained that a C-section was necessary.

"During the contractions, you see, the baby's heart rate is strong," he explained. "But after the contraction it decreases." He pointed to the chart, "See here? See how it is low here? That's after the contraction. This is not good because we need oxygen to make it to baby's brain during delivery. Sustained periods without oxygen during birth can lead to brain damage and mental retardation. I'm not trying to scare you, but you need to know that we need to get baby out now and it has to be a C-section."

Kerri's tears flowed the entire time the doctor spoke. She squeezed Simon's hand, and if she would've ever let up, he would've squeezed back. There was nothing to be done. Doctors get paid the big bucks to be right. Kerri knew this. Simon knew this.

Little Emily was born healthy as could be.

11

"You always rush off Simon," Mark said.

"You know me, man. I love my wife. I'm not going to stay at work any longer than I have to," Simon replied. "See you Monday."

Simon threw his leg over the motorcycle, fastened the chin strap of his helmet, and waited a few more seconds for the engine to warm up. He loved his motorcycle. Even with full protective gear on, there was nothing that felt as free as being on a bike. Learning how to ride one only recently, he loved how he could be alone in his head while traveling to and from work. On his way home that day, Simon thought about how Mark and the others had been asking him to stay for the last few years and he never did. He always championed that he thought it would be disrespectful to Kerri. This, of course, was also meant to convict the other husbands that they should probably get home too. Simon liked putting on airs that he was a good husband. As any secure person knows, however, a braggart is that way because of insecurity and doubt. The truth was that Simon wanted to stay more than anyone. But he knew that in staying the beans would be spilled. He couldn't hardly have a conversation with a friend without complaining about his marriage. Kerri this, Kerri that. Among close friends, a little venting now and again was acceptable, he thought. But the happy hour scene would prove fatal to his carefully crafted image of being happily married, so he raced home.

He loathed that Kerri did not even get up to greet him anymore. He couldn't understand how someone could be alone all day and not even be happy to have someone to talk to. Kerri wasn't to blame, though. It had been a long while since Simon had been worth talking to.

"Do anything besides watch movies today?" he asked.

"Uh, yeah. Raised Emily."

"Must be rough," he retorted harshly, climbing down onto the floor and tickling Emily's chubby stomach.

Kerri rolled her eyes and walked to the bathroom. Once there, Kerri purposefully lingered for much longer than needed. Not five minutes into being home and he was already goading her.

"You okay in there, babe?" he called finally.

"Yeah. Sorry. Just needed a break."

"Where do you want to go for dinner?" he asked, walking to the master bedroom with Emily in his arms. He placed her on the center of the bed and began changing out of work clothes and into jeans and a t-shirt while Kerri finished up.

"I don't know. Feels like we always just hit the same restaurants," she said.

"You know me. I'm fine with whatever, I just could use a break from decision making. So pick something," he said. "And quick. I'm starving."

"I really don't care," she said.

"You know what I hate about this argument we always have?" he began. "I hate that we always have it. Why can't you just be ready with a restaurant? You know I don't like always making every decision. You've got all day on Fridays to decide. It's not like this is a surprise meal out on the town. Every single Friday I rush home to see you and Emily while the fellas all linger and drink. What do I get for my reward? Laziness. You can't even muster the energy to pick a restaurant. I'm not asking you to cook me a five-course meal. I just want to eat out with my wife and daughter. I want to not have to do dishes. I want to see you smile when I say funny things. I want you to be impressed that I change Emily's diapers every time I am available."

Kerri shut herself back in the bathroom.

"Babe. I'm sorry. I am sorry. It's been a long week. I just want to have fun this weekend. Fuck."

He looked at Emily and immediately wished he wouldn't have cursed.

"Whatever," he mumbled.

Picking Emily up, he walked to the bathroom door.

In a baby girl voice, Simon said, "Mommy? Daddy is really sorry for what he said. More than that, he is sorry for his tone. He knows he should be grateful that you are taking such good care of me. And he knows that it isn't easy, despite seeming like it might be because I'm such a good baby. Hell, I'm the best baby the world's ever seen because of you. I'd say that all other babies pale in comparison to what it's like to be your daughter-"

The door opened.

"Emily uses 'hell' appropriately? Who taught her that?"

"Probably learned it at school," Simon answered, feeling like he dodged a bullet. "You know how they say standards are lowering these days."

"Yeah, well, she doesn't need to be using it at home."

"Got it. Can we be friends again?"

"Friends?" Kerri asked. "Hmm. As in, I have to act like I like you?"

"Unfortunately that's what it means."

"Well," she began, then turned to Emily. "I suppose I can fake it for one night."

"Fine by me," Simon replied, quickly. "I can't tell the difference anyhow."

Kerri rolled her eyes and leaned in to kiss Emily's cheek.

12

The weekend was no different than any other in the last five years for Simon and Kerri. They had money in the bank and spent it as fast as possible. While making their way up and down the aisles of all the latest big box stores Kerri would pick something up and Simon would give her a look that made her feel stupid and small. The items could have been pots and pans, maybe bed sheets, or sometimes even more trivial.

"No. No. That's where I'm drawing the line," Simon said. "What are we even doing anymore?"

Kerri looked confused at first, but when she saw Simon was serious, she became angry and said, "Are you kidding me? It's hand soap."

"It is hand soap. We're not buying new containers of hand soap every time we run out. That's a waste of money. Just get the refill. We already have soap dispensers. What are you thinking?"

A good Christian upbringing kept the volume of these public displays of contempt low, but any man born of a woman would've recognized what caused Kerri's slump as she put the soap back on the shelf.

Never one to let things be, Simon went off a little more.

"Seriously, babe. What are we doing? We go out every weekend and I watch you mope around the store while I lean on this shopping cart in toe. Is this really what you want to do?"

"What do you think?" she pounced. "No this isn't what I want to do. I want to have fun. I want to do something exciting. I want to go on trips," she began. "But we can't. We can't do those things because your job has brought us to the middle of nowhere and all there is to do is stare at this crap and talk ourselves into needing it."

"So my job? That's the cause of your unhappiness, eh?" he began. "Good theory, but there's a problem with it. You knew where we were moving. You knew!" he paused for effect. "And if I remember right, you were actually excited to move here. Do you remember that? You were excited. I even asked you, 'Are you sure you love me and this relationship isn't just about where we're moving to?' Remember that? Why would I even ask that if I couldn't tell that you wanted to come here?"

"Yeah, well. I was wrong. I made a mistake. I changed my mind."

"And, excuse me, but I'm sorry that my job, the job that I, not you, I," he pointed at his chest, "go to every day and which affords you everything your heart desires, I'm sorry that *that* job is making you just miserable. Happy with my apology?"

He saw her stare at him in disbelief.

"No? No, you're not happy? Or no you're not grateful to have food and shelter and water and spaghetti string tank tops and toasters and French presses-"

"Enough!" she yelled.

This time a customer did look over.

"Enough," she repeated, in a whisper. "Can we just go?"

"What do you think Emily? Is it time for your nap? Want to go home?"

Simon looked at Emily. Pacifier in mouth, she stared back at him with a sadness that made him uncomfortable. A look that said, "Please don't fight mommy, daddy."

****

Lifting the carrier into the back seat of the car, Simon said, "Kerri. Look. I'm sorry. But soap? How is soap going to make you, how is it going to make us happy?"

"Will you please unlock my door?" she asked.

He pressed the button on the remote and climbed in to the driver's seat.

"And, I take it, this little scene means no sex tonight? That's good. Can't wait for next Saturday now."

13

Simon and Kerri had a rule. Well, Simon had a rule. Kerri just agreed to it. Drinking was not a problem if it was not a problem. That is, when Simon and Kerri first met, besides being new to sex, Simon was also new to drinking. There should be no surprise there. Over the last few years of the marriage, though, Simon had taken to drinking quite a bit. But he remembered in college that the most accurate definition of alcoholism a team of researchers could develop was that there was a problem only when your drinking habit affects your life. For example, if a college student parties hard every night, but always goes to class and gets desirable grades, then that was not alcoholism. Somehow, for that individual, they are able to achieve a balance. Simon always liked this definition because it allowed him to deny that he had a problem.

The first few months of their relationship, maybe even as long as the first two years, Kerri would seem like herself to Simon only when they were drinking. These days, however, even tipsy Kerri would not bend. She just would not loosen up. Soon she didn't even drink anymore.

Simon, on the other hand, could now be found nearly every Saturday night alone on the lazy-boy watching his favorite concert DVDs. Not too far out of reach, and sometimes in his lap, was his whiskey. Kerri would be asleep in the bedroom, Emily asleep in her room. But Simon, Simon needed something to dull the senses. And he told himself from the very beginning that he did not have a problem. As long as he got up the next morning there was nothing to worry about, he told himself.

Kerri did not fall asleep easily on these Saturday nights. She longed to hold a man tight as much as any unhappily married woman. Letting the heels of her feet lead the way, she'd mope from the bathroom to the bedroom one final time each day in a sort of zombie-stupor. The bed was never fully made in the morning, so getting back in at night was not a long process. She laid flat on her back, pulled the covers up to her neck, and closed her eyes.

****

"You still up?" Simon whispered.

"Mmm," her response.

"It's been a week. What do you say?" he asked, kissing her forehead and hoping to move to her encouraging lips.

"Not tonight, Simon. In the morning," she said, barely conscious.

"Come on," he tried one final time.

"If you ask again, it's not happening in the morning," she said, trying anything to get him to let her sleep.

"Fine."

It wasn't fine. Simon knew the game. Emily would be the first one awake. Kerri would stick to her side all day and then be too tired to fool around during nap time. And then before he knew it, the weekend would be over.

"Hey! What are you doing?" Kerri said.

Simon had pulled all the covers to himself.

"You're such an asshole."

"Try falling back to sleep now," he thought as he happily let her struggle against his weight to get them back.

The first time Kerri said no, way back in the early months of their relationship, Simon figured he had it coming. There was no way he found a woman who liked sex—no way, he told himself. His entire life he had paid extra attention to anyone and anything that talked about healthy sex lives in a marriage. Why? Because he was waiting until marriage and because everyone seemed to say sex doesn't happen in a marriage. The most promising numbers he found were on a local news program one weeknight. Average looking people, in admittedly average sounding marriages averaged out to three times a week. Simon thought that sounded great. But his own life was proving less than average.

Every "no" carried a hurt like Simon had never felt before. It became comical to him, so he sought "no" even more desperately. He used it as justification for treating Kerri like shit. Waking up in the morning he'd make a move. He would run his fingers along her pantie line or simply kiss her cheek. Even when he didn't have time he did this. He did it just to be able to have a reason to make her feel bad that night.

"Why?" she said. "Why do you always start when you know I'm going to say no?"

"I have needs, Kerri," he said, knowing that was about as un-romantic as possible.

"Well, I have needs too. Right now, I need sleep."

"Big surprise there. All you do is sleep. All you've ever done is sleep," he said, throwing his half of the bedding onto her as he sat up and leaned over the edge of the bed. "You sleep more than anyone I know. And I was fine with that. I make enough money for both of us to have plenty. So go ahead;

sleep your life away if that's what you want. But you have to be with me at least some of the time. You haven't been with me for years. It's the same old shit over and over again," he said. Opening his mouth to continue, he hopped down from the mattress and Kerri's tears were held at bay by the baby monitor coming to life.

"I'm sorry," he said, snapping back into the reality that Kerri had a big day ahead of her.

"Fuck you," she said, waiting for him to walk to the bathroom so she could go get Emily in peace.

14

"I just wanted her to be happy. I thought I could do that," Simon explained to Will one lunch. "But I don't think that woman will ever be happy. So now I want her to feel what I feel. Isn't that messed up?"

"Yeah, Simon, that's kinda messed up," Will agreed. "Why don't you just get a divorce?"

"Ahh," Simon said, visibly withdrawing from the table. "I can't do that. Then I would be exactly like my dad. I won't do that. I won't. Plus, there's Emily. She needs two parents. I don't think Kerri could maintain if she had to raise Emily alone part of the time. Kerri knows the truth, no matter how she acts. She hasn't worked in years and wouldn't make enough to support herself, let alone Emily.

"Plus," Simon continued, "it's not like I'm saying I don't love her. I just want her to feel what I feel. I want her to feel hurt and realize that it doesn't feel good, and then after that, realize we need to change."

"Simon, I'm not sure it works like that," Will offered kindly.

"We don't sleep in the same room anymore, Will."

"What?!"

"I didn't want anyone to know but I had to tell someone. Yep. The other night she said she'd sleep with me but that she wouldn't take off her shirt."

Will wrinkled his face in disbelief.

"She wouldn't take off her shirt?"

"That's right."

"That's not right, Simon."

"Oh, I know. I'm not playing games anymore. So I said, 'Sorry babe. You just crossed a line.' And then I went to the spare bedroom. Been there all week."

"I'm sorry Simon."

"Have you ever heard of such a thing? I know this is personal, but I need help man. How do you and Julia behave?" Simon asked, a desperation showing through.

Will looked around at the other tables in the restaurant before answering. Both men knew that their conversation was quieting down the other patrons.

Not being as thrilled with everyone knowing the intimacies of his marriage, Will spoke softly.

"No, Simon. Julia would never do something like that."

"Fuck."

"Simon, that's not right."

"Well, there's nothing I can do about it. Fuck."

"You'll figure it out man. You always do."

"Thanks, Will," Simon said. "Thank you for sharing. I know I ask a lot. I owe you."

"You don't owe me anything."

15

"I was thinking about what you said, Simon," Will volunteered at the next lunch.

"Oh yeah? What part?"

"The part about you becoming your dad."

"And?"

"It's a crock of shit. You're not becoming him if you get a divorce. He had his reasons. You have yours. Two totally different situations."

"Two totally different situations that involve a more experienced woman," Simon retorted.

"Almost. But not quite. The fact that you made it this long and have Emily makes it a tremendously different set of circumstances," Will argued. "Sure, if you were only a year or two in and were still childless, I'd be ready to agree more. But you obviously loved each other, otherwise no five years, and no Emily. Right? And remember," Will added, "your dad went on to have his own family and is still married to your mom. I'm just saying that there's hope."

Simon wanted to believe that they loved each other once, but the facts just didn't seem to support that notion.

"I'm not sure it's quite that simple," Simon said. "But yes, I do—or I can—see your point. I'm still not getting a divorce. No way."

Lifting his head back from his straw, Will said, "I'm not telling you what to do. I just think you have some options. Don't suffocate yourself on imaginary restrictions."

Did Simon love Kerri? Did Kerri love Simon? Both of them asked themselves these questions daily. What is love? What is marriage? Why is divorce so appealing so much of the time? These were the thoughts Simon had, and more. Divorce. Divorce, divorce, divorce. Divorce was so prevalent it was difficult not to be always aware of its seductive power.

Simon thought highly of himself, but not so highly as to believe that he was better than the reported fifty percent of the population who divorced. What did it even mean to get divorced, he wondered?

"I can't understand why anyone gets married," said Simon's brother, Ted, one night on the phone. "Every friend of mine that is married sounds miserable. They are all checking with their wives for permission to just breathe it seems."

"Yeah, I don't know," Simon said, pretending to be doing something in Emily's room so he could have a private conversation. "In the beginning it was so different. Now I can't get the number sixty out of my head."

"Why sixty?" Ted asked.

"As in sixty more years together."

"Oh."

"Ted, seriously, how many people do we have to watch throw their lives away because of being too afraid to leave a relationship. I refuse to stop living just because of a decision I made once when I was-"

"When you were what? You there?"

"-when I was young. Sorry, I thought I heard her coming," Simon said, walking back from checking if Kerri was outside the closed door. "I was saying that I would rather be a failed husband than a miserable one."

"I don't know what you should do, brother. I really don't. I wish I did. We all do. Mom and dad see it. Jessica sees it. Even her husband Ben sees it. The thing I'm worried about, and I know you are too, is that Emily is going to see it. That's definitely no good."

"Hey, you're telling me. Talk about an unwinnable situation. I can either let Emily see a dysfunctional male-female relationship and send her into the world unprepared, or I can give her co-parents," Simon said.

"There is another option, of course," Ted said.

"Yeah, I think about that. I just don't know," he said, wondering why he was breathing hard. He realized that had been pacing pretty good for some time now. "So get this. We went to this counselor a while back. Remember the stripper thing?"

"Yeah."

"Yeah, so anyhow, we are at the counselor. No wait, back up. Before the counselor, I call my good college buddy. He tells me about a book which he claims has helped his marriage. Something about love and respect. The theory is men and women need different things, and most women don't realize they disrespect their husbands, but more than that, most women don't intend to.

"So, Kerri and I talk about it, and she agrees it sounds like a promising book. So we head over to the book store, and each grab a copy to read. It's full of Bible verses and stories etc. I'm kinda half-n-half on what I think about that, I mean just because they are in the book, doesn't mean the book's ideas are wrong or not valuable. But Kerri is more suspicious of it all, so within thirty minutes we are re-stocking the shelves and dejectedly walking to the car. There was no hope."

"That's too bad, Simon."

"Yep."

The brothers let the pause go uninterrupted for some time before Simon heard Emily laughing and said, "Well, I should get going. Thanks for talking. Thanks for listening."

"No problem. Good luck. Call anytime."

16

Simon came from a very fundamental Christian background. Consequently, despite the fact that he stopped practicing any religion years earlier, another reason he felt that he couldn't get divorced was because the Bible said it was wrong. For pleasure he was reading up on some history books about Jesus and suddenly the topic of divorce appeared. In an instant, the otherwise dry text became a page turning extravaganza. Using very sound methodologies and measures of historicity, the verdict was clear. Jesus forbade divorce.

Can you imagine what comfort this brought Simon? Almost since the beginning of the marriage the word, the way out, was in the back of his mind. But he never wanted to do it. Now, he finally had solid ground from which to proceed.

****

"You see, Will, I have never heard of higher demands on life than what Jesus requires. Never. I don't mean any of the supernatural hocus pocus, I mean the 'love your neighbor as yourself', 'love your enemy', 'turn the other cheek', and now I am convinced that he really did forbid divorce—no exceptions," Simon explained while leaning back in the chair opposite Will's desk at work.

"I don't understand where you're going with this," Will said.

"I'm saying that I found my strength. I found my guiding light. I am a very externally motivated person. You know this. I need a set of principles to stick to. Aristotle's virtue for virtues sake. Now that I am certain the most virtuous thing is to stay married, I will stay married," Simon reasoned.

Will, like he always did, looked right at Simon and waited to respond. He knew, like we all knew, that Simon couldn't allow the pause and would take the bait and explain further.

"What do you think? Am I right? You just don't know how it felt to read what I read last night. To finally have an answer."

"I guess I'm not entirely sure you stumbled upon an answer that is sustainable. Who cares what some dude said two thousand years ago? You're the one who has to go home every day. You're the one who claims that you're unhappy. I don't see why you won't fall right back into wanting to end the relationship."

"Maybe, Will. Maybe you are right. But I've got to try. I'm desperate."

"So what else is going on? You guys talking? What does she think about all of this?" Will asked.

"Well, we talk. I mean I talk. She says she doesn't want a divorce any more than I do. But then that gets depressing to say over and over again. Nobody wants a divorce, but nobody knows how to be happy. And I don't know if I believe in happiness anymore. Kerri just doesn't seem like she'll ever get there. I feel like I remember being happy, but these days it seems like I maybe was just ignorant back then."

"You ever think about trying to be nice to Kerri for a bit? And then seeing what happens?"

"Be nice?" Simon asked, rhetorically. "Sure. I think of being nice. Just as soon as she recognizes that she has a pretty freakin' great life in front of her and stops moping around and acting like the world's coming to an end. Just the other day we had the same fight about going out to eat. I can't deal with that type of stuff man."

"Okay. Okay. Calm down."

"Sorry. I just, it's just the minute I start thinking about how fortunate the two of us are living without a single want being unmet and yet she won't just be happy, I just get angry. I'm not going to be her motivator, her source of happiness. No way. That's on her," Simon said. He had become more and more animated as he ranted, eventually leaning forward in his chair. Will just sat and watched while Simon regrouped. Simon then leaned back, folded his fingers together behind his head, and began again, "Just consider how Emily was born. Not a single bill. I heard one other couple say they had twenty thousand dollars in debt from the pregnancy and delivery. Twenty thousand dollars for doing the most natural thing on the planet. We owe nothing. I never even saw a bill. Everyone is healthy. Emily is doing great. I mean there is so much that could have gone wrong and none of it did. I can't stand the word blessed, but we're blessed."

"Sounds like it."

17

I have mentioned how Simon had an unreal ability to focus on a goal. As is the case with other men with a similar skill, this intense focus could sometimes cause Simon to lose sight of the big picture.

For her part, Kerri was living an existence best described by the word numb. She didn't know what she did to deserve being treated the way Simon treated her, and yet she had an intuition based on experience which told her both what he wanted and to not give it to him.

A full on family vacation with Simon's parents soon was planned. A bustling resort town near pristine lakes was chosen and reservations made. Simon, Kerri, and Emily were the only out-of-town family, so special attention was afforded them. The relations between them were worse than anyone had previously imagined.

"I really don't care to hear these little stories you always tell, mom," Simon snapped back one morning as he sat with his mother Barbara and Ted.

"Why am I always the one who gets picked on and has to keep quiet?" she asked.

Simon didn't reply and Ted refused to make eye contact with either contender. Soon Simon saw Barbara's face reddening.

"I'm sorry mom. I don't know why I said that. I'm just in a bad place these days. Life is not going well," he said.

Lifting her head, but keeping her eyes downward as if still reading her magazine, she said, "I just want everyone to be happy. Is that too much to ask for?" She then looked directly at Simon. Ted also turned to Simon.

"It might be. I'm miserable. I don't know what to do. What am I supposed to do? Kerri's miserable. This whole thing feels like a mistake. I'm done trying to make her happy. I was done trying to do that years ago. I feel like there is only one option, but I can't bring myself to do it."

"What option is that?" she asked, uncertain and afraid for her son.

"You know, divorce."

"Oh, Simon. Don't do that. Think of Emily. Think of Kerri. There's got to be something you guys can do. Have you considered counseling?"

"They're all I think about. It's depressing. The only time I'm not ready to call it quits is after I don't think about them for a long time. That's sick, huh? We did try counseling once. We're pretty far apart though. And this ideal couple situation they talk about is just something I have never witnessed with my own two eyes. You know as well as I do that I never really wanted to be married. I just married Kerri because I liked her and thought we could have a fun life together. She wanted to be married, I didn't care one way or another about the label, so we got married. Now it seems like we made a pretty big error in judgment."

"I don't know what to say."

"I know, mom. I know. There's nothing for you to say. Don't spend too much time worrying about us. It'll all resolve itself one way or another."

"I'm sorry that you guys are going through this. Please remember that it doesn't hurt you to be kind to her."

"Easier said than done. Why should I be the one who is kind? I really don't know how to explain what it is like to live with her. I feel like all I have done is improved her life and I am repaid with the same sexless miserable marriage that everyone gets. Whatever. I don't want to talk about it anymore. Let's just try to have a good time the rest of this trip."

"Okay."

Later that week Simon, Kerri, Barbara, and his father Joel took Emily for an after dinner stroll around a nearby lake. Barbara hung behind with Kerri and the stroller which carried Emily, while Simon and Joel walked ahead.

"We're in separate bedrooms, Dad," Simon said.

Joel stopped dead in his tracks. Simon didn't need to look at him in order to know that his father had clenched his teeth behind closed lips and stuck his chin out. Simon knew that next Joel would put his hands on his hips and lean over at the waist and shake his head. Upon confirmation that he knew his dad's mannerisms pretty well, Simon urged his dad to begin walking again so as to keep their conversation from their wives' ears.

"Simon, I know I never talk much about my first marriage, but you're falling into the exact same trap. I stopped sleeping in the bedroom as well. This is no good."

Now it was Simon's turn to let his body manifest his thoughts. Both arms swung up as he turned his head to the sky.

"This is exactly what I was afraid of. You can ask my friend Will. I have been telling him that I won't be able to deal with the fact that I did the exact same thing as my father."

"You have to talk to her, Simon," Joel declared. "You have to."

"I don't think that's the ticket anymore. I have tried to talk to her so many times that I'm sick of hearing my voice. And if she doesn't want to talk, then I'm done talking as well. It seems like all my words ever amount to in her mind is evidence that I'm a bad husband and mean and cruel and on and on. I don't need to be a part of that. I'm not going to cause my own demise here-"

"Alright. Alright, alright. Just stop. Let's stop. Here, they're almost caught up. Let's wait for them and see if they want to get some ice cream."

18

Vacation over, Simon awoke to the sound of a ringing phone.

"Hello?" Simon said while still staring at his phone in disbelief that someone from work was calling.

"Hey Simon. You coming in today?" the familiar voice of his boss said on the other end.

"Yep. Why what's up?"

"Can you get here soon?"

"Sure. Is everything alright?"

"Yep. Nobody's bleeding or dying or anything."

"That's good."

"See you in a bit then."

"Bye."

"Who called, Simon?" Kerri asked.

"Work," he said. "My boss wants me to come in early. No big thing, he said. But something's gotta be up. They've never called before."

Kerri sat up in bed as Simon began to shave and shower.

Soon Simon burst through the door with a grin on his face.

"I think I figured it out," he said. "I am pretty sure they're going to let me quit."

Kerri's eyes lit up just a bit.

"Really?" she said.

"It's the only thing that makes sense. No more deep south livin' for us. We're moving up and out!"

Simon was right. His boss told him that his request had finally been granted. They needed him to stay for a few more months, but then he could go do whatever other work he could find.

"So how soon? When are we moving? Where are we moving? What are you going to do for money?" Kerri asked, realizing that the good news also carried some risk that might get overwhelming.

"I don't know all the answers yet," Simon reported that night. "but he said end of February is my last day."

Kerri tried to be happy, but soon the enormity of the change couldn't be ignored. Knowing Simon wouldn't respond well to second-guessing the decision, she fell back into a state of restraint. She didn't let herself worry too much, but neither did she allow herself to be excited for the change.

19

Simon was scared. Once again he was moving Kerri, and now Emily, to a new city. He was changing careers. I've said that we all liked Simon, but professionally, he had little to no experience with the types of jobs he was applying for. He was hopeful, but foolhardy is probably a better fit than courageous. All this is to say that Simon did not rise to fame and fortune like he had hoped, and too soon it became clear that Kerri needed to find a job as well if they wanted to stay afloat.

I haven't told you about Kerri that much, have I? Well, now is as good a time as ever, I suppose. Kerri was a beautiful woman. She inherited jet black hair from her Japanese mother, and a slim five foot six inch frame from her tall white father.

A nerdy older brother meant that she had no tomboy leanings, but certainly could enjoy a Star Trek re-run as well as anyone. I mentioned earlier that she had a knack for articulating herself, and I mention it again to prove that it isn't hard to believe that she interviewed well.

Neither Simon nor Kerri put themselves before Emily. That is one point that must not be missed. They agreed that daycares were not ideal, and since Simon already had the Monday through Friday nine-to-five job, Kerri found part time work on a few nights and weekends.

The reader's imagination does not have to be highly developed to appreciate the perfect storm that was waiting just around the corner for Simon and Kerri.

20

"She asleep?"

"Yes."

"What are you going to do?"

"Probably watch a movie. Why?"

"We're still fighting too much to have sex tonight, right?"

"Right."

"Well, I'm off to the bar then."

"Bye."

He twisted the front door handle. When it didn't open he remembered that it had to be muscled a bit. Embarrassed that he was going to a bar to drink alone while his young wife and baby slept, he looked back to pull the door closed but avoided looking inside.

He was never quite the bar type, but he was sure to notice that there was one within walking distance of the new house. Finally there'll be no need to worry about DUI's, he thought. Ever curious, he measured the distance from the bar to the house one night on the drive home from work. It was seven-tenths of a mile. Not a bad walk, he thought.

The sidewalk lined the street. The streetlights were on but didn't help Simon to see the cyclist that almost rode into him as their paths crossed that night in the darkness underneath a broad shade tree. Shocked at how close he came to serious injury, Simon stopped walking and turned back to see the cyclist grow smaller and smaller.

Picking up the pace, he walked past the last pedestrian crosswalk. He looked left, right, left again, then jogged across the street to the parking lot that had seen better days. As usual it was nearly empty.

"How does this place even stay in business?" he muttered to himself as he pulled the door open.

Simon loved to tell his friends, "It's a shit bar. I've noticed there seem to be about four regulars." He would then wait for a second and with a contagious smile, add, "I guess that means there are five regulars."

The ice was still crackling as he took his first sip. Soon he noticed that another man had pulled up a barstool. Good, I need to piss, he thought.

"If I leave this here, you're not going to put any roofies in it, are you?" he kidded the man.

"What's that? Oh, no," the man replied, shaking his head.

"Good. I gotta piss."

Returning to the same scene that he just left, Simon felt like conversation.

"So what's your story man? What are you drinking? My name's Simon," he said as he extended his hand.

"Nice to meet you Simon. I'm Richard. You can call me Rich. Double rum'n'coke. Nothing exciting. Just stopping in for a drink."

Within minutes Simon learned that Rich was married to a functioning alcoholic. Rich's wife was from a nice family and she was able to spend eight hours at work all day, but then she just drank. Drank and drank and drank and drank. Mostly vodka. Simon grew so sad.

"That's horrible man. How long have you been married?" he asked.

"Going on twenty years."

Simon felt his stomach turn. He didn't want to know any more than that. He knew that what he was doing would lead to the same spot. He could recognize a pattern. This Richard was miserable. Twenty years miserable.

"You ever think about divorce?" Simon couldn't help asking.

"Sure. But she'd never do it. Her family wouldn't allow it. And I don't want to divorce her. I'd like things to be different, but I don't want to be divorced."

21

Simon drove from his downtown office back to his house in a confused state. The ballgame started in an hour and a half and was back downtown. He knew he should've just had his friend from college meet him downtown, but it seemed like it made more sense to drive home, wait for Phil there and then take the train to the ballpark. From there he thought they could drink and talk as much as they wanted without having to risk DUIs.

And they did drink. And they did talk. And, of course, Simon forced divorce into every other topic.

"Dude, I haven't told many people, but my parents just got a divorce," Phil empathetically shared. His far-away look indicated that he was still feeling the effect of the news. "They were married for nearly thirty years. They fought a lot, but no one—I mean no one—saw this coming. And you already know about my older brother and his wife."

"Yeah. Only too well. His story filled a lot of night's conversation back when we were in college," Simon said. "I'm real sorry to hear about your parents. That's no good. What is wrong with all of us?"

"Who knows man," Phil said softly, his eyes still locked in a stare.

Phil was one of Simon's oldest friends. They went to college together, becoming roommates by the end. There was nothing they kept from each other. Perhaps this is why Simon shared something he had never told anyone before.

"Can I tell you something I haven't ever told anyone?" Simon asked.

"Sure man."

"Actually, wait. Did I ever tell you that a year ago, before we moved here, a drunk driver drove his van into Emily's room only moments after she woke up from her nap and Kerri had moved her to the living room?"

"What?! What the fuck? No, you never told me that. Was everyone all right?"

"Yeah, yeah. Everyone was alright. It was a super messed up situation. The dude lived on the inner part of the P shaped neighborhood. He was wasted and if he had turned left out of his driveway he would have simply passed our house on the right and probably killed someone as he turned onto the state highway that our neighborhood was off of. But no. He turned right out of his driveway and that meant when he circled around, he came to a stop sign at the lone T-intersection, which has our house on the other side of it. Most people, of course, stop at stop signs and then turn. Well, he must've passed out and so he didn't turn. He didn't even stop. He just took the curb, drove across the lawn, and smashed through the outside wall, then the inside wall, and finally the next wall was enough to stop the then coasting van."

"Jesus. Where were Kerri and your daughter?"

"They were ten feet away playing in the family room. Kerri said she just heard a huge crash and grabbed Emily and went outside. She looked around and saw nothing at first," Simon paused. "Think about that Phil. She saw nothing. The van was entirely in the house. As she walked towards the street there was a truck passing by that slowed and the driver pointed to the house, and that's when she turned back and discovered what the hell just happened."

"What the fuck!"

"Anyhow, I was working that night, so I came home early when I got the call. It was a wreck. And that's what I need to tell you. I'm so embarrassed about how I reacted, but I need to tell someone."

"You shouldn't be embarrassed man. Nobody handles that kind of craziness with poise."

"Yeah, we'll see what you say in a minute," Simon said, taking a breath. "Want to know what we talked about that night as we laid together in the neighbor's spare bedroom? I argued that it wasn't that big of a deal. I argued—mind you argue means fought—with her that had Emily still been in her crib, she would've been untouched as the crib was still whole after they pulled the van out. The van had gone so perfectly straight that it left all of the furniture that was grounded to the walls untouched. I actually said the words, 'Emily might have had a few sprinkles of glass on her covers, but she would've been fine' before I realized what an asshole I was being."

"Simon, you were right. That's horrible. What's going on with you man?"

"It gets worse Phil. You know that my marriage is shit right now, right? Well it was shit back then too."

"You don't have to tell me these things, Simon. I mean I'll listen, but you're in a rough spot and don't need to beat yourself up like this."

"No. I need to tell someone. After that incident I actually had the thought—my mind created the thought—that it would have been better, not better, but easier, if Kerri would've been killed."

"Jesus Christ, Simon. Stop."

"That's what I'm saying! I need to get out of this marriage. No one should have thoughts like that. I mean what the fuck? I don't want Kerri to die. Never. And yet, there I was, daydreaming of how easy life would get if fate would've intervened like that. Can you understand the nuance that I'm trying to explain? It wasn't like I was thinking, 'Man, I wish she had died.' It was that my constant concern with solving this horrible marriage problem led me to contemplate that *had* she died, I would have had my out. A no-strings attached out. Marriage over. New happiness coming soon."

"Huh," Phil mumbled as he stared through the floor of the train. "I don't know what to say. Sounds like you're in a mess."

"That's the understatement of a lifetime, Phil," Simon joked, shaking his head. "Sorry. I know that there's no response to it. I just had to tell someone. I'm so ashamed."

"It's a horrible thought to have, but that's what trauma does to people. I mean you know about PTSD, right? That's what you guys have going on after an event like that. I'm not saying it's the exact same just that you certainly don't need to dwell on retarded thoughts."

"You're right. And I don't dwell. I just think that it illustrates how miserable I am. It feels like my marriage, my family is being attacked on all fronts, but what's worse is I'm joining the offensive, when I should be leading the defense."

22

Kerri followed Simon out the backdoor as he headed to the garage.

"So that's it?"

"Yep. That's it," Simon said, nodding with a mocking smile. "I'm done. We're getting a divorce. We don't have the money to do anything quick, and I'm not mad at you, I just can't be your husband anymore. We can talk more after work, but as far as I can imagine it, the future is we live together as roommates until there is enough money for you to get a place, and then we file the paperwork etc."

What was the last straw? What finally caused Simon to break? The particular events do not matter. What matters was Simon was finally out of options in his quest to hurt Kerri. Divorce was his only play. So he played it. Kerri would surely understand the hurt he felt now, he thought.

His drive to work that morning was filled with that special rage that seems to bring joy.

"You want to be miserable? You want to sit on the couch all day long? You want to never have sex? You want to be ungrateful for every undeserved act of kindness? Well now you get to do that by yourself. Fuck you, Kerri. Fuck you," he thought, his mind racing. It's a wonder Simon didn't get in a wreck he was so focused on everything but the road. Taking his rant to another level, he actually yelled out loud to the empty vehicle. "I'm so sick of being made to feel that I'm the cause of your misery. I gave you so much. You didn't have to work a day, not a day. Well no more. We're done. I'm done. It's over. You can go be miserable by yourself," he continued. "Oh," he said, loving the ability to be melodramatic, "And guess what? I'm taking Emily. I'm not letting her be around you and your misery. The only reason you've done a good job so far is you are terrified of being perfect at fucking up every good thing that came into your life. You fucked up college, you fucked up every relationship, and now you fucked up your marriage. Well, unfortunately for you, Emily will be able to tell the difference between fear-based love and genuine compassion. She will know that you're afraid and become afraid herself, and I'm not going to let that happen to my daughter. No way. Just try and fight me on this. I dare you."

He looked up just in time to see the car in front of him was stopped and that he needed to immediately brake hard to avoid a collision. But he felt amazing. Better than amazing. He was free. He was out. He was done feeling like the bad guy, done feeling like a failure. And he might get to have sex again without it feeling like rape. And Kerri would now feel the full reality of the hurt that he wanted her to feel all those years. Things were looking up for Simon Pastor.

23

That night Simon walked to the bar with a pep in his step.

In case I haven't been clear up to this point, Simon was an asshole to Kerri for most their marriage. So how did he behave post-divorce announcement? Even worse, of course. He was totally unencumbered. He could say anything; he felt like he could be himself. There was finally no "worse thing" that could happen.

Richard was sitting at the bar when Simon walked in.

"Hey, Rich," Simon said.

"Oh, hey," Rich said. "I'm sorry, I can't remember your name."

"It's Simon. No worries. I did it man. I finally did it."

"Did what?"

"I decided to get a divorce," Simon announced. His jubilance was a little off-putting to say the least.

"Well, that's usually a terrible situation, but you seem happy about it. Congratulations, I guess."

"Terrible situation? No. Not at all. She's finally getting what she earned. You don't just get to go through life treating people like shit. Not without consequences."

The bartender approached and asked what Simon wanted to drink.

"Same as always. Whiskey on the rocks. Make it a double."

"You got it," she said as she poured.

Rich asked, "So what's the plan? Do you have any kids?"

"Plan? I have no idea. We have a daughter. I don't see how I won't get to raise her as I'm the only one with the ability to make any money. I told my wife that I'm fine with living as roommates until she gets a stable full-time job that pays enough for her to move out on her own. I want her to know she messed up, but it's not like I'm kicking her to the curb.

Obviously she is the mother of my child. That's something at least. It's probably the only thing she's good at."

"Do you have an attorney? Does she? I'm pretty sure it's not as easy as you have a job therefore you get your daughter."

"Na, we're not doing attorneys. There's no money for that. Actually, one of the ways I know this hurts her is that she is so scared she called her parents and they had two attorneys at the ready before the morning was up. It's kind of messed up, really. I don't see that there is much to argue about. We'll probably just do mediation."

24

The roommate thing didn't quite work out like Simon had planned.

Simon kept going to work as usual and Kerri kept looking for new jobs that had a better schedule. Soon both Simon and Kerri learned about the five-two-two-five. They also learned that custody isn't really a word anymore, nor is alimony. Actually, nothing was like either of them had suspected. Simon was also knocked down about four hundred notches when the mediator told him that the state law gives equal co-parenting time unless someone can and wants to prove that the other parent will harm the child. And now Kerri was acting like he, Simon, shouldn't get to see Emily much because of this and that.

Two phrases saved Simon's sanity. The first was, "You can pay for your attorney's children to go to college or you can pay for your children to go to college." The second was, well, no, there was only that one. Simon and Kerri both agreed that blowing money was not beneficial to Emily.

Simon remembered studying in college about making decisions when under duress. It was never a good thing. The law even recognized that contracts could be proven void if they were signed under duress, if he heard the professor correctly back then. And yet he and Kerri were making lasting financial and scheduling decisions as fast as possible so as to not have to pay more money to the mediator. Simon didn't see any other option so he just did the best he could. Kerri did the same.

Meanwhile, on the home front, Emily was now in daycare full time. Unintended consequences have ended wars, prevented wars, and started wars. This particular consequence shook Simon to the core. For the initial part of the separation Simon found himself dropping Emily off and picking her up from the day care more days than not. Emily's tears as the teacher pulled her out of Simon's arms were almost too much. He questioned the very meaning of life as he walked down the hallway and out to his car. Occasionally he had to reign himself in from yelling at a parent who sighed relief upon leaving their kid in the classroom. Anesthetizing nightcaps reduced the duration of each day's insanity just enough to be bearable.

Was it excellent breeding that allowed Simon to keep his rage inside during daylight hours and public situations or poor breeding that caused Simon to unleash his true rage upon Kerri every chance he had?

Can we be reminded enough that technology is nothing more than a tool? That it can be used for good and bad? I mention this now because on principle Simon refused to even purchase a mobile phone until late 2011. He preferred real contact with people. As he was unable to have that contact with Kerri anymore, he resorted to spewing his hate in texts.

25

August 14, 2013 10:00am

"The new school called, they have space," Simon read on his phone as he sat at his office.

Typing diligently and trying to play it cool, he texted back, "Sweet...how to proceed?"

Moments later he read, "I just got the message...I can't call right now, can you?" Followed by, "I just have to say it, I am conceded about the change."

Confused, Simon fired off a quick, "?" and "Conceded?"

Kerri responded--

Concerned

Great Kerri, glad to see you're not a robot...calling in a minute

Ok, next step is for one of us to swing by and fill out huge packet of info...i cam do it if you can't, she will start Monday.

and oh, let me explain something...you don't have any money, therefore you're concern is heard, but meaningless. You're just trying to keep some sort of control, but in this specific case you're clearly behaving crazy. You know this school is better, AND it is cheaper.

26

Another example of how the technological marvel aided his hurt-giving:

September 21, 2013 8:30pm

> It thrills my spirit when she tells me that she watches movies at your house

> You probably feel the same way I do when I hear someone other than who you told me would be picking her up from school. Oh, and poptarts.

Karen is better than Susan, and it was a last minute substitution. Like you know either of them. Pretty sure movies and tv rot her worse than pop tarts.

I'm just glad to see that you've finally joined the group of adults who domt want to raise their children

Whatever. I'll just wait a bit and you'll completely flip your position.

South park makes fun of parents letting tv raise their kids...your parents didn't let you watch tv, but somehow you decide that with your own child that it's best

Maybe she'll be friends with my students who cant believe a person doesn't watch tv. I'm going to so proud of her for not possessing the capacity for abstract thought.

27

October 14, 2013 12:27pm

What company will you be
working for?

Its embarrassing okay, let
me just get hired, then ill
share...working there is
less embarrassing than
applying there

Wow. You realize you're asking a whole lot? You're asking me to change my life because you didn't want to do the 2 previous jobs you had. One making rather good $. You can see why this is overwhelmingly frustrating

Well, you can always think of it like this...if you want your money, you might have to be uncomfortable for a bit. I'm pretty sure the payment would be lower if we used my new salary

Wow. Is that a threat?

No. I'm simply reminding you that im out a 1600$ for nothing, every month. That's not exactly motivation to take over the world

I don't see what one has to do with the other. And her being in school isn't nothing and the $750 is making it possible for Emily to live in a nice, safe neighborhood in a good school district so when sh'es ready for kindergarten you'll be relived of the $800/mo

to be clear, im not in a pissy mood

I do not think school is better than a stay at home mom, and im glad that the public school option is on the table

The point is, "life happens" and so the schedule needs some flexibility in the near future

I'm pretty sure I had her every weeknight without complaint this time last year

I'm not either. I'm just amazed that you don't see how selfish your actions are

That's one way of looking at it. From where im sitting, I feel like a benevolent king. And now I am getting pissy. I'm so glad we met.

For 4 months, right when we were separating and it was the only full time job I was offered. You've had 2 jobs that you quit because you didn't want to do them anymore. I haven't needed to change the schedule for a year.

You made it very clear when we were discussing the church thing that we are divorced and that means it's over and you don't have to tell me anything. Then why does my life and emilys life have to change because of your actions

Benevolent King? How's that?

I'll have supported you for 12 years. This is the only job I can get. The teaching job was less than minimum wage, and im running out of available credit. I'm sorry you can't seem to see there is more to life than money, but I won't work for someone who thing they're doing me a favor.

So, your pride is more important than providing a stable environment?

Kerri—I don't care what you think. I told you when we met. 'The only kind of respect that matters is self-respect'. It's the only thing you nor anyone can ever take from me.

And so it was that Simon began his new low-paying job in retail management.

Simon couldn't see it. Honestly, nobody could. Not Kerri, not Simon's parents, not even me. But Simon was in trouble. He was only seeing his daughter a couple nights a week, and he was drinking heavily the rest of the week. Why not? he rationalized. He had nothing better to do. He drank. He thought about the facts. He silently raged.

28

Email sent May 24, 2014, after a hard day of work at another new job.

You're pure white trash. I thought we were meeting about the schedule. Only when I was nearing absolutely out of money did I begin a discussion with you about easing up on money stuff. You on the other hand lie about why you want mediation and then reveal your true agenda is simply that you know I finally have a decent paying job and you want more money. Bitch.

Sincerely yours,

Your former husband, Simon

29

Text June 5, 2014

11:11am

Have you ever stopped and realized that nearly every time we talk its you wanting / needing / spending more money? Wtf? I don't owe you jack shit. There's a name for women like you, you know. I'm pretty sure you had a t-shirt once that said it. Not once, not ever did you even try not to divorce. And yet you think you're owed a certain type of financial stability? What's wrong with you?

30

September 10, 2014 11:34am

Is there any way I can convince you to take her to school at least on one of the days this week?

I'm only seeing her for one and a half day as is. (Tuesday and Thursday til 3). I miss her.

I told her on Thursday that she's starting the new school on Tuesday. She's been talking/asking about it all weekend.

Well, on earth, parents decide things, not kids.

31

October 23, 2014 4:51pm

> I'm not fine with paying any more than the cheapest option, which was the last school.

> You don't stick to anything we agreed to. We agreed on 50/50 which hasn't happened for the last 2 months.

And apparently won't be
for another couple m

Months

You need to decide what
your problem is. I know
where I stand. The only
reason I am working this
shitty job is because you
think I owe you something
because I decided I
couldn't stand living with
you anymore. I didn't and
still don't think that it's
cheaper or worth paying an
attorney vs. paying you
what I don't think you
deserve. If you don't want
to help raise your child (I'd
pay to spend more time
with her) that's your
problem.

I know 4 divorced women. You're the only one who demands payment. And now you're the only one who is trying to squeeze out more payment.

Wow. You have absolutely no grasp of reality.

By my count I have decreased the amount of money you have to spend.

Hmm...stay at home mom = free. Daycare plus maintenance equals $1500+ a month.

Hope you like your job

Hmm what about your infidelity and addiction? Don't think I agreed to that

If you think you're so justified in your assertion that you shouldn't have to pay me, let's go back to mediation and see if you are correct.as a part of the deal.

This is the difference between me and you. You think there are rules to a breakup. I do not. You brought in maybe $5k, if that. You have no claim to any assets. I'm done paying other men to appease you. There is no reason for mediation. You're going to get your hard earned money. I'm going to have learned the hard way to trust my gut on women. At least we're both getting something out of the experience.

32

November 6, 2014 3:09pm

I'd rather have her all the time, but I know you are important to her. My life is built around her, so when you dictate when I can see her because of your schedule, it sucks.

Each of us is a capable parent. That means we each get to be with her for half the time. You're not doing me a favor by "letting me" see her. Nor am I doing you a favor. I don't understand where you are coming from like I don't build my life around her. I do. This is exactly what I mean when I say that it feels like you think there is a competition. It's not like she's "yours" anymore than she's"mine". Do your best. I'm doing mine. She's doing hers.

And you will forever be the one who checked out of the marriage first, so I'm in no way responsible for telling you when you can see her.

You could've been raising her all day everyday. I'm the one who was always going to have to work.

It's pretty messed up that you talk like you do about Emily. She could hate my guts and I still get her half the time. You don't own her. Your relationship with her isn't the "main" one. Your not the "actual parent." You don't even see her much. The nanny is raising her when she's with you. A stranger. And that she spends anytime watching movies when she's with you is even more time you're not raising her. Great job. But she knows not to smack when she eats. What would she do without you?

Lastly, it's difficult to get an answer outta her, but we tried a shower the other day, and in the discussin that lead up to it, I couldn't tell for sure, but she alluded to the fact that your boyfriend is around during bath time. If that's true, that's wrong. Only parents or immediate family get bath time. He's a stranger. She's almost too old for me to help with the bath. So stop that if you've let it happen. It's not right.

33

November 20, 2014 7:16am, after Kerri hung up on Simon.

> You know, I tried for six years to make you happy. It's impossible. You're a user up miserable woman. I'm certainly not trying after we divorced.

> Used*

> And I'm not a narcissist.

Do you ever think what kind of example you're setting for her when you live with a man out of wedlock? You want her to be like you?

Does he enjoy living off of another man's incomce?

Porn addiction, cheated on her mother with stripper when she was 13 weeks pregnant?

That's all you have...hold tight to it

Oh, I have more. I'm not worried.

Try me

Provided you more money that you'll ever see again? Took you out of your shitty town. Educated you? Fixed your eyesight?

Two attorneys on call within a half hour of the word divorce

Can't live by yourself

Can't support yourself

Lived with your parents at 25

Is Emily ready for when you break up with this guy? That's what I'm dying to know

That's what bothers me most, to tell the truth. You put her in so deep so fast with these strangers. She doesn't remember that last women I dated. She'll remember this guy and his mom and the little girl. You're going to be the one who introduces real innocence lost to her. Are you ready for that?

How do you feel when you think back to asking me to meet you at the restaurant so you could tell me your grand scheme to piss 20$k away on school and move back with your folks? How long had it been between boyfriends? Two weeks? A month? Don't even try to call me names while you're living off me like a leech.

And Emily can most definitely here you droping eff bombs from the bathroom. Why does everyone think houses are sound proof?

34

It is probably strange that I have not had much of a voice in this story of Simon Pastor's road to divorce and doom. But the honest truth is that I failed him. And I am embarrassed. I was closest to him and even I did not recognize just how lost Simon was. And by the time I did, it was too late.

I got a call from Simon on the night of December 14th, 2014. He asked if I was still awake and had time to come over and talk. He had never asked me to come over on short notice before. I grabbed my jacket and headed over to his place.

Simon opened the door and I could smell whiskey on his breath. He looked like a crazy man.

"What the fuck, Simon? Are you okay?"

"I saw it," he said.

"Saw what?"

"I saw the future."

"What are you talking about? You're drunk. Let's stop drinking, stop talking nonsense, and start sobering up. You've got to work tomorrow," I said, trying to be the calm one.

"No!" Simon yelled, pushing my hand from his shoulder. "I'm not letting you stop me."

"Stop you? What are you talking about? I'm here because you asked me to come over. I am your friend."

He lifted his arm into the air towards the top of the refrigerator and he grabbed his plastic whiskey bottle—he always drank the cheap stuff. I noticed another unfamiliar bottle sitting next to it. I couldn't figure what would be in such an odd little container and why he would put up there too, so I walked closer.

"What the fuck is that Simon? Is that poison? Oh, no. You're not killing yourself, buddy. Not on my watch."

"You don't know what I've seen Pete. Why do you think I called you? You want to write, right? Mr. Big Blogger? I'm sorry, Captain Big Blogger. Captain I-Always-Have-Something-To-Say," he mocked.

"Enough Simon. I don't know that I can beat you, but I am not going to stand idly by while you kill yourself tonight."

Saying that I pushed him back and down to the floor as hard I could. He was slower to react than if he had been sober, but when he hit the floor I saw his eyes flash rage.

"Oh shit," I muttered.

He must've noticed me look up to the poison and guessed my plan. He quickly dove at my waist and lifted me skyward. He had the advantage of strength, passion, and being numb to pain. I thought I saw my chance to grab the bottle while he swung me around, but I missed it and next thing I knew I was accelerating towards the kitchen floor.

"It's got to stop!" He cried out. "I've got to stop. I saw where this leads."

I picked myself up and tried to pretend I was not going to fight again, but when I made a move his fist landed squarely on my ear.

"Simon, stop! What are you doing?" I yelled, crying.

"You're not listening, Pete. I have to do this. If you won't watch, then get the FUCK OUT!" he screamed.

He picked me up again and try as I might I couldn't get out of his grasp. At first I braced for another trip to the ground, but then I noticed he'd been walking for too long. I started pounding on his back with everything I had. My blows had no effect.

"No, Simon. Don't throw me out. Don't. I'll watch," I lied. "I'll watch. Just don't lock me out. I'm your friend."

It was too late, he had the door open and in an instant I was against the apartment's hallway wall in a heap.

The door slammed shut.

I had seen too many movies to call for help. It never comes. Simon's life was mine to save and mine alone. Kicking the door as hard as I could with my heel only hurt my heel.

"SIMON!" I yelled. "LET ME IN! I can help you. We can get help. You don't have to do this!"

I heard glass break against the door.

"FUCK OFF!" he yelled.

I needed to get in that door. I needed something heavy.

"There's a bowling ball in my car!" I remembered.

Running to my car I returned with the ball in hand.

THUMP!

The deep sound of wood giving way echoed down the hallway. A neighbor's door cracked open, but quickly shut when we made eye contact.

I used both hands to smash the ball against where I thought the deadbolt would be and felt the wood give way again. One more time and the door cracked open.

Simon pulled the door the rest of the way and landed another punch square onto my nose. I stumbled back and my own adrenaline pumping, I felt a competition growing inside me.

"You want to fight? You want to hurt me? Is that what you want? You sick of hurting Kerri? Now you want to hurt me?" I chided.

This time I ducked as he labored another right hand toward me.

I countered with a left hook and caught him by surprise. I had only one goal. Knock him down long enough to get to the fridge. He didn't go down, but he did stumble and so I threw a right. It glanced off his cheek, but before I could attack again he hit me in the stomach so hard I crumpled to the floor. I gasped for breath as I saw him grab the bowling ball with a look of curious fury. Before he could use it against me, I kicked at his knee as hard as I could and he finally fell to the ground. I had my chance. Running to the kitchen I reached for the bottle and realized something was not right. My hand wouldn't work. I had broken it at some point.

"Pete. Don't. Please don't. You don't know what I saw."

Reaching with my left hand, I grabbed the bottle. It was empty.

I turned to see blood coming from the corner of his mouth. He didn't even try to wipe it. He coughed.

"I tried to tell you, Pete. I saw the future. I don't stop. I don't stop hurting Kerri," he cried. "Oh God!" he exclaimed.

"And to do that, I hurt Emily. It has to end this way. It had to end this way. I don't want to hurt anymore."

"No, Simon. What have you done? What are you saying?"

"You have to tell my story, Pete. You have to. Emily will need to know. Kerri needs to know."

I walked over to him and he grasped my pants as he coughed up more blood. I instinctively backed away. Suddenly I realized he was done fighting and needed help right then.

"Come on Simon. How much did you drink? We'll get you to the hospital and fixed up in no time," I said, mad at myself for crying. He slowly stood up and had his arms around my shoulders. I tried to turn us sideways, as he loudly coughed into my ear.

"Let's go Simon," I said, weeping. He went limp and pulled me to the floor with him.

"SIMON!" I yelled. "I love you! I need you. You can't leave me."

He opened his eyes and looked at me.

"There you are. Come on buddy. I need you to stand up."

I couldn't stop crying.

"Once we get to the car you can relax."

The blood landed on my face. I wiped it and my tears away as best I could and placed his arms over my shoulders for a second time. He nuzzled his chin around my neck.

"It's okay," I soothed. "It's going to be okay. Just stand up with me."

"Pete."

"Yes, Simon, I'm here."

"Pete."

"Simon, I'm right here."

35

The funeral was outside, cold, and windy.

Emily sat next to Kerri in the right front row, that is, when she wasn't getting restless. Simon's mom wouldn't let anyone sit next to her in the left front row, not even the preacher. Joel sat with Ted instead, one row back. The rest of the family and friends fell in behind them. Everyone wore black.

The turnout was larger than expected. Simon had made an impression on quite a few more people than he ever would have imagined.

I tried to hide in the back for as long as I could, but eventually Phil came up to me and said, "Pete. We've all been talking. It's not right to let this service conclude without hearing from you. Please say something."

"I wouldn't know where to begin," I replied.

"That's a lie and you know it," he pressed. "Please. It's just not right."

"Fine."

As I walked to the front, I could feel the crowd's eyes follow me. I told myself to not look at Kerri or Barbara or Emily when I turned around. But, of course, I did.

I squeezed the sides of the portable podium as hard as I could and tried to stop crying. I saw Simon in each person's eyes as I surveyed the crowd for someone to help me regain composure.

The longer I stood in silence, the quieter the crowd became.

"Why's everyone so quiet?" little Emily asked, breaking the silence.

"Shh, Emily. Come here," Kerri said, reaching for Emily and putting her on her lap.

Of course it would be Kerri, I thought to myself. She looked me in the eye and moved her head. It wasn't much. Just a little knowing nod.

I finally gathered myself and said--

"Men get stuck."

The End

About the Author

Pete Deakon served in the Air Force for eight years as a Captain and pilot before settling upon a career as a writer. He publishes daily blog posts on his Captain's Log which can be found at www.petedeakon.com.